# Old MELROSE, St BOSWELLS and BOWDEN
## with DRYBURGH, GATTONSIDE, MAXTON, MERTOUN and NEWTOWN St BOSWELLS
*by*
Judy Olsen

This postcard was sent in the summer of 1907 and shows the centre of Melrose, looking up High Street to Market Square. Thomas Paterson's shop can be seen in the distance, to the left of the Market Cross. The building on the left with the crest is the Masonic Lodge, believed to be the oldest in Scotland. The lady on the right is about to pass Anderson's Temperance Hotel (now Burt's Hotel). Further up is the Ormiston Institute, with its large clock bearing the date 1892 and a plaque explaining that the building was erected by the trustees of Charles Walter Ormiston of Eildon Grove, Melrose, who died on 14 January 1882. Nearby is the Corn Exchange, where in October 1898, Thomas S. Smail of Jedburgh performed his amateur ventriloquial sketches at the Foresters' Soirée, and recited 'Bob Banks' Botherment' by request. In 1898 it was decided to pave the south side of High Street with concrete and, from the photograph, this work appears to have been done. The streets are lit with electricity; in February of 1904 the *Jedburgh Gazette* reported that: 'On Monday evening an explosion occurred at the newly erected electric works at Melrose belonging to Messrs Crompton & Co. The Company use gas as motive power, and make it on their own premises. One of the gas bags exploded, and Mr Richards, the manager, received serious injuries to his head. David Screen, fireman, was also rather seriously injured.'

Text © Judy Olsen, 2005,
First published in the United Kingdom, 2005,
by Stenlake Publishing Ltd.
Telephone: 01290 551122
Printed by Cordfall Ltd., Glasgow, G21 2QA

ISBN 1 84033 293 X

**The publishers regret that they cannot supply copies of any pictures featured in this book.**

### ACKNOWLEDGEMENTS

The author wishes to thank the many local people who provided information and recollections, including: Mr & Mrs Gordon A. McLaren of Mertoun Bridge, Mrs Carol Chisholm of Jedburgh Library, and the residents of Gattonside. Thanks also to Rootsweb 'listers' who shared information and family stories, including: Valerie Henshaw of Australia, Nancy McLaughlin of New Zealand, and Adeline Martin and Catherine Furlich of the USA.

### FURTHER READING

The books listed below were used by the author during her research. None of them are available from Stenlake Publishing. Those interested in finding out more are advised to contact their local bookshop or reference library.

G.A.C. Binnie, *The Churches and Graveyards of Roxburghshire*
Bowden Kirk Session, *Bowden Kirk 1128–1978*
John W. Butcher (ed.), *Around Melrose*
Anne E. Campbell, *Old Gattonside*
Charles Denoon, *Maxton 2000*
Norrie McLeish, *Borderline Cases*
Melrose Historical Association (ed. D.M. Hood), *Melrose 1826*
Charles Alexander Strang, *Borders and Berwick: an illustrated architectural guide to the Scottish Borders and Tweed Valley*
*The New Statistical Account of Scotland* (1845)
*Rutherfurd's Southern Counties Register and Directory* (1866)
*The Statistical Account of Scotland* (1791–1799)
*The Story of a Community: Dingleton Hospital, Melrose*

# INTRODUCTION

The town of Melrose occupies a delightful location close to the banks of the River Tweed, between the distinctive peaks of the Eildon Hills and the sunny slopes of Gattonside across the river.

In the first half of the twelfth century, King David I, the great sponsor of the Border monasteries, invited Cistercian monks from Rievaulx to the Borders. They originally settled at Old Melrose, the site of a much earlier religious house founded by St Aidan, but soon moved upstream, diverting the river and building a lade to power their mill, and quarrying for building stone in the Eildon Hills.

A town grew up around the abbey, just as houses and businesses clung to the skirts of the old Roman fort high above it. The oldest settlement in Melrose was probably Little Fordel – between High Street and the abbey entrance – but once the Reformation took hold building began to encroach further northwards into the abbey environs.

The river provided power for milling, fish for food, and a handy drain for the abbey's waste. Later on the fish would provide the bait for a new source of income – the wealthy visitors who built or rented palatial sporting lodges in the vicinity. The banks of the Tweed were a popular retirement spot for former soldiers and colonial servants who had made their names and fortunes in India.

Perhaps the most famous and influential resident of the area was Sir Walter Scott, who built a mansion a few miles west of Melrose at Abbotsford, using the services of the local builder and architect John Smith. If Scott was the publicist for Melrose, Smith was its architect – building everything from bridges to the colossal statue of William Wallace at Bemersyde.

Drinking water for the abbey came from a spring above Dingleton and the monks installed lead pipes to bring it down the hill. Private residents of Melrose relied on draw wells until the 1830s, when a pant well was installed, with a tank inside for storage and a trough provided for animals. Since residents could pay for piped water from 1838, the pant well was in use for a comparatively short period.

Across the river at Gattonside were the abbey's famed south-facing orchards and their importance is still recognised in the ceremonies of the annual Melrose Festival. Until October 1826, the residents of Melrose and Gattonside needed to cross a ford to visit each other, but a new chain bridge allowed them to cross the Tweed without getting their feet wet, and is still in use. Its tollhouse also survives.

The history of the abbey itself is a sorry tale of attacks, repairs and wilful neglect. After vicious English raids in the fourteenth century there was extensive rebuilding and it is impossible to be sure if the abbey was ever really completed. After the 'Rough Wooing' of Henry VIII and the abolition of the monasteries came lay Commendators, re-distributing abbey wealth whilst allowing the buildings to be robbed of stone and lead. After the Commendators, the lands fell into the hands of the local nobility.

For a couple of centuries, the nave of the abbey was pressed into service as a parish church – rough and unpaved and thoroughly unsatisfactory to people who still believed that disease was spread by damp air and smells. The architect of the replacement church was the young John Smith of Darnick, who was also on hand to help when Sir Walter Scott started to direct repairs to the abbey in 1822. A century or so later, in 1921, came a discovery that Scott would have relished: a leaden casket found under the Chapter House floor contained an embalmed human heart – possibly that of King Robert the Bruce. The casket was re-examined in the 1990s and reburied in 1998.

The parish church was by no means the only place of worship in Melrose. The eighteenth and nineteenth centuries were a time of religious dissent and the earliest Secession Church in Scotland was founded at

*Opposite:* At the time of writing, Thomas Paterson's old premises in Market Place, Melrose, were still being used as a grocery shop and the vestiges of the Paterson name were still visible on the fascia. According to the 1841 census, which does not specify relationships between inhabitants, Thomas Paterson, grocer and ironmonger, was living in Main Street with Margaret Paterson and nine children, including Isabella (aged four) and Thomas (aged two). In Rutherfurd's 1866 directory Thomas Paterson is listed as a grocer and wine merchant in either High Street or Market Place, the two being listed together. A Thomas Paterson, aged 40, was listed as a wine merchant in the High Street in 1881 and the business was still listed in the Edinburgh Post Office Directory for 1924/25. Isabel Paterson, 'last surviving daughter of the late Thomas Paterson, wine merchant, Melrose', died at Trinity in Edinburgh in September 1909. A son, William – 'Mr Paterson of the Glen, Langholm' – went into the brewing trade at Longtown Brewery and died in June 1896 at the age of 72.

Midlem after the Duke of Roxburghe imposed a minister in the parish of Bowden.

Until the late-nineteenth century local government for a place like Melrose came in two main forms – the parish and the burgh. Both were potential power bases for local tradesmen and landowners who might also serve as magistrates, overseers of the poor or a Commissioner of Supply, with wide responsibility for transport infrastructure and tax collection.

Melrose Cross was a focus for town life and the symbol of its status as a burgh, with the right to hold markets and fairs. It was also the starting point for the annual Fastern's E'en ball game, a boisterous tradition that other Border towns tried to ban without success. In Melrose the objectors prevailed and the game has not been played for over a century.

The community shown in these photographs had recently been introduced to a more modern style of local government. Commissioners of Supply were superseded by county councils in 1889 and heritors' meetings were replaced by parochial boards and finally by parish councils.

Before Melrose Station opened in 1849 the fastest way to travel from the capital had been by coach along turnpike roads – goods went to and from Edinburgh in wagons and outlying places were served by local carriers. This did not mean that the roads were safe – runaway horses, drunken carters and bicycles were all potential hazards.

The pictures also show a country town with little in the way of industry. In the mid-eighteenth century Melrose weavers were producing 30,000 yards of linen a year but this success was short-lived and the linen bleachfield was eventually turned into pasture.

This lack of industrial development helps to explain why early twentieth century Melrose is so easily recognisable. This book also includes intriguing views of some of the surrounding mansions, and the smaller villages and communities which surround the town. In some cases it has been possible to identify not only places, but individuals, and their names have been included wherever space has allowed.

*Opposite:* Symbol of the town's status as a burgh, the Market Cross retains its centuries-old design although its shaft and finial are recent replacements and the base dates from the mid-nineteenth century. The Melrose contributor to the *New Statistical Account of Scotland* was delighted that, 'The Popish emblem on the top, however, was supplanted by the crest of the Haddington arms as early as 1604'. A quarter acre of land, known as the Corserig, was let out in return for keeping the cross in good repair. The iron fountain was in use until the 1930s and replaced a hexagonal 'pant well' which held water piped down from the hills and included a trough for animals. The tobacconist's window advertises Mitchell's Glasgow Tobaccos and Prize Crop cigarettes – a member of the same Mitchell family moved into Monksford House at around this time. The narrow street past the Ship Inn leads to the town's East Port and former tollhouse. In 1905 the *Jedburgh Gazette* reported how a young lady in a dogcart took fright when a motor car appeared in Market Place. The car was travelling at a reasonable speed, but as the young lady was trying to get her vehicle out of the way her fear overcame her and she fainted on the bottom of the cart. She was conveyed to a chemist's shop and soon recovered.

This postcard of Melrose Cross and High Street was sent in early 1909 and shows Market Square, looking west with the High Street in the background and the gas lamp beside the Market Cross still in place. The British Linen Bank on the right was built in 1897, probably to replace buildings destroyed by fire. In February 1898, it was decided to purchase a burgh fire hose, which was put to good use on Wednesday, 5 July 1899, when High Street suffered another serious conflagration. The flames spread rapidly through workshops and stores and gunpowder kept in a house was removed in the nick of time. The walls of McDonald's workshop were left standing in a dangerous condition and the Burgh Surveyor, Adam Morris, was supervising their demolition when he was hit by falling masonry. He died on the Sunday evening, leaving a widow and a large family. A public inquiry was held and the Morris family lodged a claim for £1,200 against the Melrose Burgh Commissioners. The imposing building on the left of High Street is the George and Abbotsford Hotel, previously the George Inn, where Sir Walter Scott stayed with the Wordsworths in 1803 – Sir Walter and William had to share a room. In June 1911 yet another fire started in the dwelling house above the bank, destroying the roof and the top flat.

With Priory Farm on the right of the picture, this view shows the mill lade which powered the abbey mill which is just visible behind the gate in the middle of the picture. Water was diverted into the lade by a cauld on the Tweed and, as well as powering the mill and another at Newstead, the system provided drainage and water for the abbey wash house. Behind the trees on the left is Harmony Hall, built in 1807 by Robert Waugh, a former joiner, who named the house after his estate in Jamaica. The parlour was panelled in cedar and Waugh supplied similar wood for Scott's drawing room and library at Abbotsford. Local opinion disapproved of Waugh's links to the slave trade and this might explain why he retreated behind the high walls of his mansion, earning the nickname 'Melancholy Jacques'. Robert was the youngest child of James Waugh, a Melrose shoemaker. His brother John also had a Jamaican estate, named Melrose, where he died in 1794 of a 'putrid fever'. Robert Waugh died unmarried in 1832, leaving most of his assets to four nieces, the children of his late sister Janet and her husband George Broomfield. Harmony Hall is now in the care of the National Trust for Scotland.

John Wood's 1826 plan of Melrose and Gattonside shows Abbey Park as the property of Captain Stedman – and that he also owned the Greenyards, a tract of former abbey land where the game of 'rugby sevens' was invented. Captain James Stedman of Broomhill was married to Sophia Mercer, and the couple engaged in extensive land and property transactions. Whilst they had bought the Greenyards together, Abbey Park originally belonged to Sophia in her own right. The Captain died at Abbey Park on 24 January 1832. Sophia outlived him by nearly half a century, and died in 1881 at the age of 94 at Heriot Row, Edinburgh. Abbey Park is now part of St Mary's Preparatory School, founded in 1895 by John 'J.B.' Hamilton and his wife Mary. At the annual school games in 1898, Mr W.H. Dunn was the judge of a full calendar of events including 'throwing cricket ball', bicycle races, the sack race and various sprinting events, and the prizes were presented by Miss Aimers. Mr Dunn remarked that they had also '. . . had a very successful cricket season, had lowered the colours of Merchiston and Loretto, and one small boy had made a score of 82, not out.'

Gladswood is an early nineteenth-century pavilion house in the parish of Mertoun, overlooking the Tweed and Old Melrose. In 1817 the estate was put up for auction and according to an advertisement in *The Times* placed at the time, '. . . the Mansion-house is elegant and commodious . . . the garden consists of more than an acre, well laid out, with a good wall, and the fruit-trees are in full bearing; the stables, coach-house, and offices of every description are new, and built in the most substantial manner.' Gladswood also came with 270 acres – 'all enclosed and highly cultivated' – a cottage, a farmhouse and fishing rights. In 1858 John Meiklam purchased Gladswood from the trustees of the late Lieutenant-colonel Spottiswood. His daughter, Julia Adeliza, wished the house to be sold on her death, but not to a radical or a Roman Catholic. When told this was not possible, she left the house to one of the sons of the Duke of Buccleuch, Lord John Scott, who sold the house in 1914 to his brother Henry. Lord Henry Scott is listed at 'Gledswood' in the 1924/25 Post Office directory, around the time he had a brush with death due to streptococcal blood poisoning. His life was apparently saved by a new medical treatment which a neighbour – Colonel Mitchell – had read about in the *Edinburgh Evening News*. Miss Meiklam also left money towards a motor lifeboat, which was named after her parents.

The Edinburgh 1924/25 Post Office directory lists Monksford House near St Boswells as the residence of Lieutenant-colonel Alexander Mitchell. Colonel Mitchell, who also owned Tulliallan Castle in Fife, was a member of the Mitchell coal mining dynasty. He was married to Meta Mary Paton, the daughter of John Paton of Lethangie in Kinross, and in the 1901 census the couple is shown living at 'Moorfield' in St Boswells with their baby son Harold (later Baronet Mitchell) and six servants. Monksford was built as a 'hunting box' around 1906, with plenty of stabling and an estate running to more than 250 acres, including grass parks, woodlands, and Norton Hall Farm. It was clearly used as a family home, since in 1908 Mrs Mitchell advertised in the *Scotsman* for a resident governess for a boy of nine ('must teach Latin, French and mathematics well'). Lieutenant-colonel Mitchell commanded the Fife and Forfar Yeomanry in the Gallipoli campaign and became chairman of the Alloa Coal Company and the Alloa Glass Works Company, and Master of the Lauderdale Hunt. He died of prostate cancer in December 1934 and the house was put up for sale soon afterwards.

In 1866 *Rutherfurd's Southern Counties Register and Directory* described Ravenswood as being 'On the south side of the Tweed, opposite its junction with the Leader – the property and residence of George K.E. Fairholme, Esq. of Old Melrose and Ludgate, Galashiels. Ravenswood was built in 1827; in 1859/60 an addition was made to it on the east end, and another addition is now in course of erection on the west end.' By 1881 Ravenswood was the home of Admiral Sir Henry Fairfax KCB. He and his wife were well-known benefactors in the area, gifting the village of Newstead a mission hall, reading room and library. In June 1899 the Provost, Magistrates and Commissioners of the Burgh of Melrose presented Admiral Fairfax with an illuminated address, congratulating him on his appointment as admiral in command of the fleet at Devonport. The address concluded with the wish that '. . . after your term of command is over, you may be spared to spend with Lady Fairfax at Ravenswood, your beautiful home, anchored as in a haven of rest, a happy, peaceful, and lengthy life amongst us and all your friends.' Despite this sentiment, Admiral Fairfax died at Naples the following March. His will included money to provide a piped water supply to Newstead.

In 1905 St Aidan's United Free Church in Melrose was the scene of a terrifying accident. A carriage belonging to Mr Henry Kidd of Lowood was being driven to Melrose Station when the horses shied at a furniture van and bolted. The vehicle was dashed against a lamppost near the church and the coachman thrown from the box seat and badly bruised. This wasn't enough to stop the horses. One of them fell in the Weirhill Road, giving the groom the chance to jump off, but they then carried on as far as the station where they broke through a gate and finally came to a stop. Unfortunately, one horse broke a leg and had to be destroyed. The original Melrose Free Church was built in 1843, the year of the Disruption, and was swiftly followed by a school and a manse; the church in the picture was built on the same site in 1852 and the manse replaced in 1883. A later fall in numbers was blamed on emigration. The United Free congregation united with that of the Parish Church in 1946 to form Melrose St Cuthbert's Church, and St Aidan's was eventually demolished. The site is now occupied by houses.

This view of Melrose and Weirhill shows St Aidan's Church on the left. The Parish Church of St Cuthbert's is prominent on its ridge behind the Greenyards and the Gattonside Heights are in the background. Weirhill was described in Rutherfurd's Directory of 1866 as 'a new western suburb of villas'. Melrose Abbey also served as the parish church and in 1618 a church dedicated to St Cuthbert was formed within the eastern nave and monks' quire by putting in wooden galleries and a stone roof to replace the existing one of lead and wood. One of the most colourful of the parish ministers from this era was Thomas Forrester whose eccentricities included inventing his own liturgy, driving livestock through the church and pressing the communion table into service as a peat cart. He was eventually dismissed in 1638 for Popish tendencies. By 1803 the deplorable and unhealthy state of this makeshift parish church was remarked upon by Dorothy Wordsworth, who called it 'the ugliest church that was ever beheld'. Shortly afterwards a new galleried church was begun on the present site to the west of Melrose Abbey. Designed, like so many of the town's most important buildings, by John Smith of Darnick, its square plan can be seen on maps from the mid nineteenth century – but the new building lasted less than a hundred years. During repairs in 1908 it burned down, leaving little more than the tower surviving. The church in this view is its replacement.

This view of Melrose and the abbey shows Dingleton Road, which leads up the hill towards Melrose Golf Club. This is now on the route of the St Cuthbert's Way long-distance path, which begins at Melrose Abbey and continues through the Eildon Hills to the village of Bowden. At the bottom of the hill on the right is Mavis Bank, shown on the John Wood map of 1826 as the home of Miss Mercer. Beyond the golf club lies Dingleton Mains; in September 1899 the local paper noted the death of a cow on the farm at the remarkable age of 28 years. She had had a total of 24 calves, and was always a 'splendid milker', giving five to six gallons of excellent milk daily. For the last two years of her life she 'enjoyed a well-earned rest, feeding on the best of everything, and using her accustomed stall in the byre'.

When the Roxburgh District Asylum opened at Dingleton in 1872, official attitudes to mental illness had just undergone a major revision. Until that time there had been little real provision for the insane. Wealthy patients could hope for a place in one of the royal asylums, but pauper lunatics had to rely on the parish or their nearest male relative and many ended up in the poorhouse. Border lunatics had been accommodated at Millholme House, Musselburgh, in grossly inadequate conditions – without even the benefit of chamber pots – but in 1872, 62 male patients and 62 women arrived at Melrose by train and were taken up the hill to their new accommodation. Admissions from 1873 show patients suffering religious excitement, domestic broils, self-abuse and softening of the brain, but there were many whose diagnosis was simply 'not known'. Elderly and mentally handicapped people began to be admitted and by 1880 the hospital was grossly overcrowded, but by 1908 building work had increased the capacity of the hospital to 440 beds. In 1992 Dingleton was earmarked for closure. Its services were transferred to other units and the site was sold for housing.

Built in 1869–71 and extended in 1876, the Waverley Hydropathic was not a traditional stone construction, despite its appearance, but one of Scotland's first mass-concrete buildings. Its location at Skirmish Hill was the site of the bloody battle in 1562, when Sir Walter Scott of Buccleuch made a failed attempt to rescue a teenage King James V from the Earl of Angus – an event chronicled by Walter Scott in the 'Lay of the Last Minstrel'. The medical superintendent at the Waverley Hydropathic from 1869 to 1873 was Alexander Munro, an Evangelical Union minister with a dubious MD from the New York Hygeio-Therapeutic College. Munro seems to have compensated for his lack of qualifications with personal charisma and social concern. Hydropathy was only one of the many alternative disciplines available to prosperous Victorians. Each patient would be given instruction in exercise and good diet, and there was a complete absence of drugs, including alcohol – the 'usual restorative' of so many Victorian accidents and emergencies. The strict regime may have eased by October 1898, when the Waverley Hydropathic was the scene of the glittering occasion of the Roxburgh County Ball. Music was supplied by Herr Iff's band from Glasgow and the catering by the Central Hotel, Edinburgh. The building is now the Waverley Castle Hotel.

In 1897 an avenue of lime trees was planted across St Boswells Green to commemorate Queen Victoria's Diamond Jubilee. The children and the photographer are standing between the first two trees at the end of the avenue, close to what is now the A68. The road now has a pavement and the view behind the children has been obscured by road signs. The row of villas is known as The Croft. A report in the *Kelso Mail* of April 1832 shows that school inspections are not a new idea. The school at St Boswells, taught by Mr Dickson, was examined by a committee of the Presbytery of Selkirk. The children were learning English, Writing, Arithmetic, English Grammar, Geography, Latin and French, and 'their knowledge is such as to surprise those who remember the school education of former days'. The notice was signed by five ministers – including Thomas Jolly of Bowden and Peter Craw of St Boswells – along with James French, Student of Divinity and Captain James Sibbald, RN. At the far end of the road is the Public Hall. The weathervane bears the date of 1892, but the cost was such that a grand concert was held in November 1896 to help reduce the debt on the building. The event was held under the aristocratic patronage of the Earl and Countess of Dalkeith and featured both professional and amateur artistes. The hall still bears a pair of gas lamps on brackets, installed to commemorate the coronation of King Edward VII in 1902.

Jutting out across the pavement in St Boswells' main street is Eildon View, which in 1901 was the home of George Melrose, a clothier, his wife Agnes and their nine children. According to local residents, the building has been at various times a bank, a fire appliance store, a florist's and an exotic pets shop. On the right of the picture is Ballantyne's grocers and wine merchants. In 1901 Walter Ballantyne and his family were living in a ten-roomed house called Oaklea: the previous year his brothers had challenged him over the estates of his mother and father, also called Walter, and the case had reached the Court of Session in Edinburgh. During the 1920s and 1930s the business flourished and in 1932 Walter E. Ballantyne, son of Walter junior, attended the annual conference of the Scottish Grocers' Federation, and contributed to the debate on of the threat posed by the Co-operative movement – which today has a large shop in the building on the far right of this picture.

Looking westwards in St Boswells, the building at the foot of the hill is the church hall, built in 1911 to replace Lord Polwarth's Mission Station which was situated elsewhere in the main street. On the right is the draper's shop of S.E. Stirling & Son. In the 1901 census, 75-year-old 'Stewart Erskin' (actually Stuart Erskine) Stirling is shown living in 'Main Road' with his 78-year-old wife Mary, sister-in-law Annie Lawrie, and niece Mary S. Davidson, a foreign missionary. Also in Main Road was Thomas Lawrie Stirling, employed as a draper, who lived with his wife, two young daughters and niece, Mabel Cranston. Mary Stirling died in 1910 and Stuart Stirling succumbed to senile debility and cardiac failure in July 1911. Thomas Stirling was a pillar of the community – a member of the parish council and a skip of the St Boswells Curling Club – but in 1933 the shop and dwelling-house were sold from under him by public roup, along with another dwelling-house inhabited by Miss Ellen Richardson at a rent of £14. These three properties went on sale at an upset price of £900, which was dropped to £800 and then £700. The sale was carried out under 'the powers contained in a bond and disposition in security' – suggesting failure to repay a debt. Thomas Stirling died in Edinburgh in 1946 at the home of his daughter Mary.

News of the surrender of Pretoria reached Scotland on Tuesday, 5 June 1900, and was transmitted to the Border towns by wire and telephone. Within hours of the announcement the celebrations were in full swing – in St Boswells this included an illuminated fancy dress cycle parade and a torchlight procession with soldiers and cavalry. Effigies of Kruger and Stein were displayed and there was a bonfire and fireworks on the Green. The figures at the front of the procession are probably representations of leading British military figures, such as Baden-Powell and Lord Roberts. The picture gives a good view of St Boswells Green, said to be the largest village green in Scotland, and in earlier times the scene of two notorious fatal incidents. In 1849 a young man named William Lauder was killed in the course of a serious riot at St Boswells Fair. Dragoons were called out from Edinburgh and two Irishmen were subsequently tried at Jedburgh for their part in Lauder's death. One of them was executed, although it is now thought he was innocent. On 12 August 1869, a hot day, the body of washerwoman Jessie Rankine was found in a well in a garden. She was the wife of John Davidson, a fisherman, and the pair had previously lived at the Maxton Tollhouse. Jessie had drowned and also had a wound to the head – since most of the well was covered by an old door it seemed unlikely she had fallen in by accident. John Davidson was tried for murder at Jedburgh, but found not guilty.

A similar view to that on page 18, but slightly later in date since the house on the left, Briarlaw, now has a hedge, and the house in the centre has gained an extension. In the 1950s this was the tailor's shop run by Loudon Melrose, who also played the organ in the parish church, and the house on the far left was Grossart's fancy goods shop. On the right of this picture is the garden gate of Laburnum Cottage; in the years between the world wars, rooms here were often let to visitors. The person who sent this postcard had recently arrived in the village and St Boswells Fair had taken place the previous Saturday – the date was always 18 July unless that happened to be a Sunday, in which case trade and festivities were held over to the next day. Rutherfurd's Directory of 1866 described the fair in its heyday, when visitors arrived by specially scheduled trains. Sheep and lambs were sold first, followed by cattle; horses were sold from about noon and wool from 1 p.m. Bank agents were in attendance to help oil the wheels of commerce and St Boswells was known as 'the great settling place for lime and manure accounts'. The afternoon was devoted to pleasure and the purchase of ready-made shoes and household articles.

Looking northwards across St Boswells Green to the historic Buccleuch Arms Hotel. The authors of the *New Statistical Account of Scotland*, published in 1845, were dismayed at the availability of strong drink in the parish: 'There are no fewer than six inns or alehouses in the parish, and without doubt, however well regulated, they present far too great a facility to dissipation.' The number of inns was not, however, enough to satisfy the thirst of fair-goers. In August 1859, Thomas Hall of the Spread Eagle Inn in Kelso was brought before the Justice of the Peace at Melrose for having sold 'excisable liquors' at St Boswells Fair the previous month. Having paid a smaller fine the previous year, Hall was required to pay the full statutory penalty of £10. Another Kelso innkeeper, Alexander Buddo of the Red Lion, was fined £2 10s. for a first offence. On Saturday, 2 June 1906, Thomas Grinham of the Buccleuch Arms Hotel had a serious cycling accident on his way back from Melrose. He lost control of his bicycle on the 'Eildon Brae' and, whirling down with increasing speed, crashed into a hedge. Dr Wade of Melrose, who was passing at the time, discovered that Grinham had a dislocated knee joint and a dangerous wound to the head, caused by colliding with a telegraph pole stay. The victim was carried to the house of Mr Alexander Hall and later in the day was taken to his home, still unconscious.

A view of the Avenue at St Boswells. In 1871 Alexander Waugh of the Green Inn decided to move to England. The sale of his hunting horses, livestock carriages, and his furniture was conducted at St Boswells Green by public roup. The sale included three hunters, a stallion, a brown mare, a milk cow, two fat pigs and a maltese goat. Mr Waugh also owned 'several' phaetons and dog-carts. A sale of horses at the Buccleuch Arms in 1902 shows that the local gentry were enthusiastic riders, but in 1913 the *Scotsman* noted that St Boswells Fair had lost out to the auction marts, and '. . . with the increasing popularity of the motor car, the show of light-legged horses has been much restricted.' In July 1935 a Dundee lorry driver named Craig Duncan was found guilty of speeding near St Boswells Green. Describing the Roxburghshire police patrols as 'rather hot stuff', he claimed he had never gone above 29 miles per hour and had stopped at St Boswells to watch the cricket before the police challenged him. However, police evidence stated that the accused had driven from Lilliards Edge at speeds of between 40 and 45 miles per hour and Duncan was given the choice of a £2 fine or ten days' imprisonment.

This picture shows the edge of St Boswells Green, on the Jedburgh side, with the road to Maxton in the background. The children in this picture are believed to have been members of a gypsy family. Travelling people are still much in evidence at the annual St Boswells Fair; in the mid-nineteenth century gypsies were known for selling crockery there. A gypsy coronation at Yetholm in May 1898 was a popular event. The *Jedburgh Gazette* reported that outsiders would be coming from Tyneside and the banks of the Clyde to sing 'Wha'll be King but Charlie?' in honour of the king, Charles Rutherford. Brakes were to leave the Royal Hotel in Jedburgh at 9.30 a.m., returning '. . . from Mr Rennelson's at 7 p.m. Return fare 2s.' There was to be a public dinner with toasts, and sports and dances to follow. The Royal Carriage was to be drawn by six donkeys, but according to the *Gazette* there was a problem finding animals to hire rather than buy – 'Donkey-owners are men of business, and know how to grasp the skirts of happy chance.' The paper adopted a jocular tone whenever the gypsies were mentioned. The following December Robert Rutherford – 'Prince Robert of Yetholm' – appeared in Galashiels Police Court for being drunk and disorderly. Although 'the royal exchequer was empty', the Prince had a job in hand to shaw (trim) turnips. However, his request for time to pay was refused and he was '. . . conveyed to the "royal apartments" downstairs.'

The writer of this postcard was staying with Miss Quarry of Deanburn, St Boswells, in the summer of 1921. Ten years later, in December 1931, the *Scotsman* reported the death of Mr William Quarry, Deanburn, aged 86. Despite his years, he had 'stood stoutly with the protesters' who aimed to protect the 'ancient Braeheads roadway' above the Tweed. The picture shows one of the village's most substantial homes, Inchdarnie House. When the house was advertised for a summer let in 1903, it was described as having four public rooms, eight bedrooms, a servants' hall, stabling for two horses and a 'small garden'. When the house was up for sale in 1926 two of the bedrooms had become dressing rooms, while another two were bedrooms for maids. The stables had gained a coach house and there was a tennis court and park – in all around three acres, looking south across open ground. This was the tennis court first used by the St Boswells Tennis Club, which later moved to the site of the old curling pond at the southern end of the Green. Inchdarnie still stands, but its gardens and orchards are now covered with streets and houses.

In July 1899 William Park junior of Musselburgh staked off the putting greens and teeing grounds for a new nine-hole golf course at St Boswells. He reported that the ground, which was part of the Lessudden estate, was most suitable for the purpose: 'The turf is very good . . . while the nature of the soil is sandy. There are sufficient hazards on the course in the shape of hedges, trees, and pools, and the river, which runs right along the course . . . . It would not cost £100 to put the course in playing order.' The golf course already had 70 members by the time it was opened by the Earl of Dalkeith in late August 1899. The Earl drove the first ball with a 'silver-mounted cleek', which he was given as a memento. According to the *Jedburgh Gazette*, he remarked that '"St Boswells is unquestionably a fashionable place in the summer, and it is therefore essential that facilities should be afforded for such a fashionable pastime as golf" (Applause). He was safe in saying that for an inland course the one they were now opening at St Boswells could scarcely be excelled (Applause).' An exhibition foursome was played and tea and refreshments were provided by the ladies in the pavilion. St Boswells Brass Band also played.

According to Alexander Jeffrey in *The History and Antiquities of Roxburghshire* (1864), 'In the end of the last century and the beginning of this, Eldun Hall [*sic*] belonged to Thomas Mein, who formed the plantations which are now so great an ornament to the place.' By the 1830s, the house had passed to the Henderson family, but in June 1832 the *Kelso Mail* reported that Mr William Ramsay Henderson, son of the deceased Alexander Henderson Esq. of Eildon Hall and Warristoun, had died at Edinburgh on 29 May. Henderson, who was only about 21 years old, left the residue of his estate for the 'advancement and diffusion of the science of Phrenology' and the William Ramsay Henderson Trust exists to this day. The estate was put up for sale, but it seems to have taken several years and a drop in price before 'Eildonhall' was bought by Walter Francis, fifth Duke of Buccleuch. Eventually, it was decided that the Duke's heir, William Henry Walter, should live at Eildon Hall in winter and spring, and major additions were made. In 1866 Rutherfurd's Directory noted that Eildon Hall was 'in the Elizabethan style, the property of the Duke of Buccleuch' and 'preparing for the residence of William Henry Walter, Earl of Dalkeith, the eldest son, an MP and Lord Lieutenant for the County of Dumfries'. By 1881 the Earl was in residence with his wife Louisa and five of their eight children.

In 1819 the fifth Duke of Buccleuch came into the title aged thirteen, following the death of his father in Lisbon. Although he kept a pack of hounds at Dalkeith he wanted kennels for his hunt near his lodge at Eildon. In the *New Statistical Account of Scotland*, the St Boswells' entry outlined the importance of this development: 'His Grace the Duke of Buccleuch has recently erected a very handsome hunting establishment to the north of St Boswells Green, which forms the only modern building of a public nature (with the exception of the church) deserving to find a place in this description.' The *Jedburgh Gazette* of 5 November 1902 reported on the opening meet of the season – the Duke of Buccleuch's hounds '. . . ran by way of Eildon Hall, passing quite close to the mansion-house, and turning south by way of the lake, where Reynard found an open earth close to Greenend. Terriers were quickly at work, and hounds were drawn off to give Reynard a chance. The fox was once again on the move, and a merry chase he led the field down the burn to near St Boswells . . . he was bowled over quite close to the public road.' The buildings have now been converted for residential use.

Thomas Munro Munro [*sic*], a former East India Company surgeon, died at Benrig House on 15 March 1862, leaving the estate to his brothers, Lieutenant-general Duncan Gordon Scott and Rear Admiral George Scott of Wooden. Other beneficiaries included his 'reputed daughter', Miss Mary Munro of Moray Place, Edinburgh. The 'property and residence of Benrig' was sold by auction in June and purchased by William Brownrigg Elliot Esq. In July 1889 Benrig suffered a disastrous fire and a few days later W.B. Elliot wrote to the *Scotsman*, praising the efforts of those of 'all classes and both sexes' who strove to save the contents of the house. The lawnmower is possibly one of Shanks's hand, pony and horse machines, made in Arbroath and available locally from 'all the leading Ironmongers and Seedsmen'. Benrig's other innovations included a private gas works and a donkey-driven pump which supplied water from a nearby spring. Both these structures have recently been restored. William Brownrigg Elliot died at Benrig on 14 July 1900. His son, William Gerald Elliot, a professional actor, seems to have inherited the family interest in politics; a newspaper report of 1910 describes the celebrations in Jedburgh following the election of the Liberal candidate, Sir John Jardine. 'Mr Elliot of Benrig said he had got the news at the station and had run all the way up. He observed on Friday that around St Boswells and Melrose all the dogs were wearing the Unionist colours (laughter). The Unionists had got the dogs at this election (renewed laughter and cheers).' Later in the proceedings, 'A voice called for "Three Cheers for the little man from India" and these were given.' This was probably a reference to Gandhi, who visited Britain in 1909.

The church in the picture is the former St Boswells Parish Church. Its remains are still clearly visible in Benrig Cemetery, about one kilometre from the present-day village of St Boswells. In the eighteenth century the village moved to its present site due to repeated flooding, but the church remained at Benrig. The minister at Old Benrig from 1789 to 1810 was John Scade, a short man who preached energetically whilst standing on a stool. He once exerted himself so much that he fell off and was confined to his bed. About two years into his ministry, John Scade was able to move into a fine new manse, which can be seen on the left of the picture, but still found that '. . . the church is not in the most centrical situation for the conveniency of the parish.' In 1940 the parish church was finally moved to the former Free Church in St Boswells' main street. The roof of the old church was removed and the walls reduced to about 40 centimetres.

This view of Newtown St Boswells shows the road leading up from the railway station, with Newtown Mill in the centre of the picture on the Bowden Burn – a corn mill here was once used by tenants farming the Melrose Abbey lands. A recruiting poster has been fixed to the gate of the local police station, now a private house. Despite the peacefulness of the scene, the calm of Newtown St Boswells was sometimes broken. In March 1898 Richard Donelly and Sarah Murray or Donelly, both tramps, were up before the Hon. Sheriff Skead in Jedburgh for a breach of the peace in the village. According to the *Jedburgh Gazette*, they had assaulted P.C. William Graham, 'by resisting him in his duty, kicking him, striking him on the leg with a walking stick, and biting him on the finger.' The pair had many previous convictions and received prison sentences of 60 and 30 days respectively. In September 1905 James Killoh appeared at Jedburgh Sheriff Court accused of having assaulted William Pringle, a labourer, within the gas works near St Boswells Station. Pringle, who had a history of drinking, had lodged with Killoh, but found himself locked out when he fell behind with his rent. On 26 August he went to see Killoh, who allegedly hit him between the eyes and knocked him down. Augustus Quinn, labourer, saw Pringle come out of the gas works with blood streaming from his nose, and helped him wash his face in a stream. Killoh, a former soldier and a member of the Edinburgh Police Force, denied that Pringle had even been in the gas works during his turn of duty. He was found not guilty.

When this picture was taken, the church at the top of the hill was Newtown St Boswells United Free Church. The congregation began as a secession church in the 1770s; the building shown was opened in 1868 and transferred to the Church of Scotland at the union of the churches in 1929. The bell came from Bowden Free Church on its closure and is inscribed, 'Gift to Bowden Free Church by benefactress Mrs Grieve 1879'. The minister from 1844 to 1874 was David Lumgair, who was long remembered for his pastoral care during the 1849 cholera epidemic which killed one in twelve of the local people. Newton Mill can be seen on the left. The Memorial Hall in the foreground bears the inscription: 'This building is erected in loving memory of Major the honourable Robert Baillie by those who knew him and among whom he lived. "A man full of faith and of the Holy Ghost" 1888.' The Memorial Hall was a popular venue for meetings and conferences, such as the annual business meeting of the Border Council of the Church of Scotland Young Men's Guild. According to the *Jedburgh* Gazette, the 1899 meeting heard from the Rev. Mr Macara, on furlough from India, who spoke on the problems of missionary work, including '. . . the difficulty of gaining anything like a thorough acquaintance with the natives. The average European treated the native with supreme contempt and made no effort to understand him; and this fact was in itself an obstacle to the success of the missionary.'

The authors of the St Boswells chapter in the *New Statistical Account of Scotland* were clear as to the advantages a railway would bring: 'A railroad either from Dalkeith to Galashiels, or from Berwick to St Boswells' Green, both of which lines have been surveyed and favourably reported of, would greatly tend to the improvement of land, the increase in manufactures, and the rise of rents.' In the event, the station was built at Newtown St Boswells, possibly at the urging of the Duke of Buccleuch. For many St Boswells passengers the distance had to be covered by cab, as an advertisement from March 1898 makes clear: 'GEORGE HENDERSON, Cab Proprietor, The Green, St Boswells, begs to intimate to his Customers and the Public that his MACHINES will now be waiting outside St Boswells Station Gates. Ordered Machines within the gates as usual. Telephone 916.' Henderson was in court that same month as a witness in the case of John Hair, contractor, Newtown St Boswells, who was charged '. . . with having on 18 February, near the Railway Hotel, Newtown, gone about in a state of intoxication, cursed and swore and used abusive language to George Henderson, cab proprietor. [Hair] pleaded not guilty, saying it was only a bit of chaff.' He had previous convictions and was offered either a £2 fine or ten days imprisonment.

This view of the Railway Hotel at Newtown St Boswells was taken from near the engine shed. Although the station and the railings on the left have gone, the buildings in the picture are substantially unchanged. In April 1933 Roxburghshire Licensing Court considered a petition presented by Alexander Bunyan of the Ship Inn, Melrose, and supported by 66 signatures. The applicant had special permission to run a bar on sale days at Messrs A. Davidson & Sons' Auction Mart, from 11 a.m. to 3 p.m., but wanted to extend this by an hour. Chief Constable Morren pointed out that the same issue had been discussed a few years previously, but it had been felt that an extra hour would be unfair to local hotelkeepers. After hearing from Mr Bunyan in person, the committee refused the petition. On the wall of the hotel is a sign for the Royal Automobile Club. Just visible on the wall near the archway is the name of the National Bank, founded in 1825, and eventually absorbed by the Royal Bank of Scotland. On the right of the picture are the premises of T.J. Featherstone, baker and confectioner.

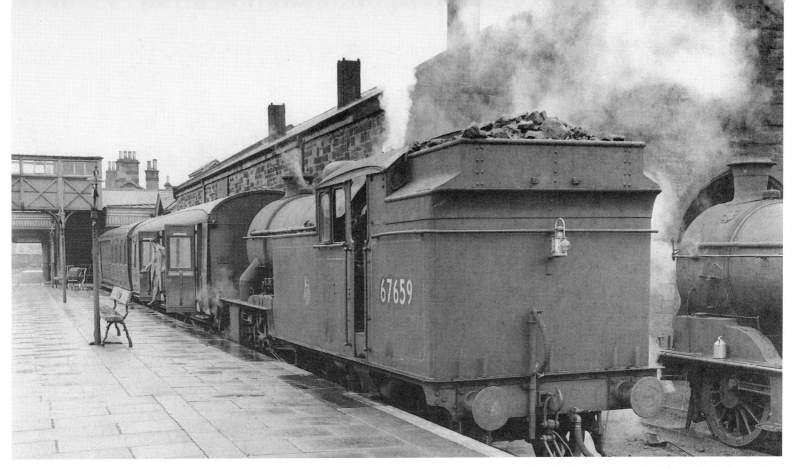

A serious accident happened at St Boswells Station in the spring of 1898, when a surfaceman named David Bain was knocked down during shunting operations. The wheels of some empty cattle wagons having passed over his leg, he was taken to Hawick Cottage Hospital where Dr Hamilton and Dr Adamson amputated the leg at the knee. In May 1899 a Mrs Stavert was travelling with three children on the morning train from Jedburgh to Edinburgh when her little boy fell out of the carriage at Merwick, between Maxton and St Boswells. According to the *Jedburgh Gazette*, 'The mother was naturally much excited, and but for the strong arm of a fellow passenger would have jumped out after the child.' When the matter was reported at St Boswells the train was sent back to pick up the boy, who was not seriously injured. On a busy day in the summer of 1908, a clerical oversight cost stationmaster John Little a fine of £1. William Mitchell, a butcher in St Boswells, was charged at Edinburgh Burgh Court for consigning a diseased pig to Edinburgh without a license, in contravention of the Diseases of Animals Act. Mitchell pleaded ignorance and Little said his chief clerk had overlooked the matter since Mitchell's pig had arrived only a short time before the train departed. St Boswells Station has long since been demolished, but the engine shed survives as an oil supply depot.

The Green at Bowden lies at the western end of this former weaving village and the small fountain bears the inscription: 'In memory of Thomas Brunton, MLC of Victoria Australia Born 1831. Died 1908. Erected by his sons'. Brunton was born on 25 June 1831, the son of Walter Brunton, a land steward and farmer, and his wife Christina Smail. After leaving Melrose parish school, Thomas became a baker's apprentice, then set off for Australia. Arriving in Melbourne in 1853, he failed to make his fortune in the gold fields, took a job in the gas works, and then became co-owner of a bakery. By 1868 Brunton was successful enough to build his own flour mill and eventually founded Australian Flour Mills. He was member of the Legislative Council for the Southern Province from September 1890 until 1904. In 1898 his health began to fail and by 1903 he had handed most of his business over to his sons, and taken up breeding cattle, horses and Shropshire sheep. He died in Australia on 7 September 1908, survived by three daughters and three of his five sons.

Bowden Manse is situated down a quiet lane a little way from the village and dates from 1794. The Rev. William Balfour moved in a few years later and was a popular and sociable figure, although his sermons seem to have been particularly tedious. A regular customer at the Red Lion Inn, he often entertained his mother-in-law at the manse, and when escorting her home was apt to trip and stumble – on one occasion losing his lantern in the Bowden Burn. To the east of the manse is Bowden Church, which belonged to Kelso Abbey at a time when the husbandmen were required to provide the monks with labour and supply them ale and chickens at Christmas. The present kirk, with its ornate Laird's Loft, is about 400 years old. Repairs were carried out in the late eighteenth century and a major restoration project took place in 1909. This was the manse that the Rev. Thomas Jolly occupied as minister from 1829. He was much stricter than the Rev. Balfour, particularly with regard to regular attendance at church, avoidance of strong drink, and observance of the Sabbath.

This postcard sent in 1910 from Bowden shows 'the Square' at the centre of the village. The gabled building in the background is the school, built in 1831 when Thomas Jolly was parish minister and John Scott was parish schoolmaster. The octagonal building is an enclosed well, dating from 1861, and just out of sight on the right is the sixteenth-century Mercat Cross, later restored for use as Bowden's war memorial. The *Jedburgh Gazette* of 9 July 1898 reported 'A freak of Nature' at Bowden – 'A white water vole (commonly called a water rat) has been caught by a cat in this district. It is a real albino, being creamy white, with pink eyes, and is being preserved.' The group of children may well include Jeanie Wilson, Isabella Ormiston and Maggie Donaldson, who were among 500 prizewinners in an essay competition organised by the Scottish Society for the Prevention of Cruelty to Animals in 1906. The prizes were presented in the Synod Hall in Edinburgh.

Mrs Grant's post office and grocer's shop in Bowden appears crammed with knick-knacks and postcards. Helen Grant had already been in Bowden for more than 20 years by 1881, when the census shows her as a widow and grocer, living with her son George, a joiner. The 1901 census again shows her as a grocer, now aged 70, living at the post office with her fifteen-year-old granddaughter, Helen Wood Grant, a letter carrier. On the occasion of her golden jubilee as a shopkeeper and member of the kirk, she was presented with a purse of sovereigns and a silver tea service. The plaque on the right marks the building as the birthplace of the poet Thomas Aird, author of 'The Devil's Dream', and was placed in 1902 by the Edinburgh Border Counties Association. Aird was born on 28 August 1802 and, coming from a family of 'anti-burghers', he would have worshipped at the Midlem Original Secession Church rather than at Bowden Kirk. After Bowden and Melrose parish schools, he attended the University of Edinburgh, which is probably where he met his friend Thomas Carlyle. Despite attending theological classes, Aird turned to a literary career, and from 1835 to 1863 served as editor of the *Dumfries and Galloway Herald*.

On the left of this view is Bowden Free Church, which was situated at the east end of the village. Mrs Grant's post office can be seen on the right. At the time of the 1843 Disruption, the Rev. Thomas Jolly became Bowden's Free Church minister. He appears in the 1851 census with his wife and four children, among them seventeen-year-old Catherine, who died of consumption in August 1863 while on board a steamer from Gladstone to Brisbane. The Rev. Jolly died in 1859, followed soon after by his wife. On 8 January 1898 the *Jedburgh Gazette* reported that the 'annual Christmas tree for the children connected with Bowden Free Church was held on Saturday afternoon . . . . Every child received a present off the tree, which was beautifully decorated, from Miss E. Brodie, Southbank, who has taken a great interest in the Sunday school for many years. Votes of thanks were accorded to all who had contributed to the tree, and to the teachers for their trouble. After a hymn was sung, and Mr McArthur had pronounced the benediction, each child on retiring received an orange and a tract.' In July the same year the *Gazette* also reported that the children of the Free Church Sunday School had their picnic to Camieston '. . . in a field kindly granted by Mr Wilson. The children were driven in carts. The weather being fine, a most enjoyable day was brought to a close by a short address from Miss Slessor, missionary, on her work at Calabar. Hearty votes of thanks were given to Mr and Mrs Wilson, and to the farmers for the carts.'

In 1895 Roxburghe Estates advertised the tenancy of the house farm of Faughhill in the parish of Bowden. Its 852 acres were about half arable and half sheep pasture. The farmhouse, which was described as 'most beautiful and very commodious', enjoys wonderful southerly views and stands in front of a much older range of farm buildings. By 1914 Faughhill was the residence of Mr James Ballantyne Stewart, whose son was born there in that year. Stewart was a prominent member of Roxburgh County Council and chairman of the police committee. In 1933, as reported in the *Scotsman*, he proposed that the county police should be given a patrol car. The vehicle he had in mind was a Alvis 16.95 'Silver Eagle', which could be had for the special price of £500. Mr Roberton of Morebattle Tofts thought that a fast car was not necessary. Provost Fisher of Hawick believed it would be useless, due to all the bends in the local roads. Major Marshall of Cherrytrees was worried that the police might become 'speed merchants themselves – like those he had seen in Edinburgh'. Mr Stewart lost the vote and the police got a cheaper car.

At Dryburgh a bend in the Tweed creates a curve of land which to this day is imprinted with the personality of one man – David Erskine, the eleventh Earl of Buchan. Erskine bought Dryburgh Abbey House in 1786, and along with it the abbey, rescuing it from a local farmer who had been carting away the dressed stone. David Erskine lived at Dryburgh until his death in 1829, creating an extraordinary legacy of varying usefulness and taste, including the suspension bridge, the orchard and its gates, the Temple of the Muses, and perhaps most famously, the eight-metre-high Wallace statue, carved in 1814 by John Smith, and once apparently painted white. In 1790 he became a founder member of the Society of Antiquaries of Scotland and 1791 he formed the 'Ednam Club' to promote interest in the work of James Thomson, author of 'The Seasons'. He was also influential in the creation of the *Encyclopaedia Britannica* and partly responsible for the growth of an early tourist attraction by granting the rights of sepulchre that led to Sir Walter Scott's interment at Dryburgh Abbey. Dryburgh Abbey House was rebuilt in 1877 in red sandstone. It should not be confused with the nearby Dryburgh Abbey Hotel, formerly known as Mantle House.

According to a lengthy obituary in the *Jedburgh Gazette*, '. . . no visit to the land of Scott was regarded as being complete without a call on Tom.' This signed photograph was posted in 1907 and shows him seated on the wall outside his house at Dryburgh. Tom Fox was born in Morebattle in 1824 and, as a teenager, was employed as a collector of the pontage (bridge tolls) at Dryburgh, but when the old suspension bridge was blown down in 1840 he took an apprenticeship as a joiner. An accident at work forced him to use a stick and a crutch for some years, but from 1849 he was back at Dryburgh as a boatman ferrying tourists over the Tweed – including, on one occasion, the Prince of Wales. When a new suspension bridge was opened in 1872 Tom was once again put in charge of the pontage. Birds flocked round him as he made his way from his cottage to his 'box' at the bridge, taking crumbs of bread from his hand. Since just about everyone who visited the abbey had to cross the bridge, Tom amassed a store of tales about famous visitors and became a celebrity in his own right. His obituary quotes his remarks to one visitor, Dr Carnegie, on the subject of some 'pilgrim lasses' – 'Yen o' them got me doon tae a meeting where she was speakin' aboot the flude coverin' the highest mountains. When she cam' in next day a' asked if she kenned that to cover the Himalayas in forty days it wad require to rain over 700 feet in twenty-four hours. It must surely hae been an awfu' splash.'

After crossing the bridge, visitors to the grave of Sir Walter Scott walked along the river bank and up the path to the abbey, straight past Tom Fox's front door. When the bridge charges were removed, he set up in business selling souvenirs and refreshments from a small hut. In this photograph he is in the doorway of his shop, where he had a superb view of the river and the Eildon Hills. Tom was a skilled woodworker and carver, and made fishing rods and fretwork ornaments as well as dressing fishing hooks. This postcard was sent in 1908, around the time the shop was burned down – Tom was ill in bed at the time. Tom's house too is now gone and the site of the hut is a small parking area. The tower on the left – complete with 'cannon' in the battlements – belongs to Stirling Towers, an ornate pair of cottages built to house the estate gardeners. The name may be a reference to Walter Scott's poem 'The Lady of the Lake' – 'King James the while, with princely powers/Holds revelry in Stirling Towers'. Aged 85, Tom Fox died at Dryburgh in January 1910 from chronic bronchitis and cardiac failure.

The re-alignment of Gattonside's main street has changed this scene almost beyond recognition, but the post office survives and is now Pergola Cottages. One of the village's best-known former residents was Mrs Lizzie Dickson – born in Earlston in the 1850s, she served as postmistress and letter carrier for more than three decades. The bicycle propped up against the fence appears to be brand new. It has a small bag behind the saddle for tools or a rain cape, and a tyre inflator. The *Jedburgh Gazette* of 8 July 1899 noted that, 'Purchasers of new machines, fitted with Dunlop tyres, should remember that they are entitled to receive, gratis, a nickel-plated inflator complete with clips for attachment to the machine'. As part of Melrose Parish, Gattonside is linked to the town by a pedestrian suspension bridge. Its south-facing slopes were chosen for the abbey orchards and in the early twentieth century the ford frequented by the monks was still used to take coal and heavy items by horse and cart. Prominent locals included Sir David Brewster, the inventor of the kaleidoscope, who lived at 'Allerly'.

This picture was taken in the east end of Gattonside, beside the old smiddy where followers of Bonnie Prince Charlie reputedly had their horses shod. The little girl is Gladys MacDowell, who continued to visit Gattonside until the 1970s. She told residents that this picture was taken in 1906, when she was twelve years old. The 1901 census index shows a five-year-old Gladys Mary McDowell, the daughter of a butler, living with her parents and three siblings in Windmill Road, Hampton-on-Thames; the postcard was sent to Master Leslie Atkinson of Hampton-on-Thames in 1907. The peacefulness of Gattonside was in danger of being shattered in the spring of 1898 when a young Englishman named Herbert Hawkins was brought before Jedburgh Sheriff Court for having had 25 gelatine dynamite cartridges and 63 detonators in a field at Fauchope Mains without a license. Hawkins was offered a £2 fine or 7 days' imprisonment.

The man in the picture is almost certainly James Dodds, who was headmaster of Mertoun School for nearly a quarter of a century. Mertoun School Board minutes show that he was appointed as interim schoolmaster in December 1879, becoming 'schoolmaster of this parish' the following July. The minutes of 13 October 1913 state that, 'Mr James Dodds intimated that on account of failing health he desired to resign his office of Headmaster. With much regret the resignation was accepted.' The entry in the school log book for the same day states, 'Today Mr Dodds resigned his position as Teacher in Mertoun Public School having been Head Teacher since December 1879.' Since Dodds also served as School Board Clerk it seems likely he wrote both entries himself. He retired to Mertoun Cottage in Yetholm, the village of his birth, and died in November 1920. His wife Annie Rodger died in December 1925. Their elder son, Trooper George Dodds of the 21st Lothian and Borders Horse, had died at Haddington in January 1916, while Howard Herbert Dodds, their younger son, died at Yetholm in 1935. The family is commemorated in a memorial inscription in Yetholm churchyard.

On a dark but moonlit morning in December 1944, a bus taking munitions workers from Kelso to a factory at Charlesfield, near St Boswells, approached Mertoun Bridge from the Berwickshire side. The driver missed the narrow entrance of the bridge and the bus plunged 45 feet down the embankment, coming to rest upside down in a stream. James Hinnigan of Orchard Park, Kelso, was killed, along with his niece, Lena Brannan of Floors. The injured were: Eva Miller, May Hill, Mrs Nisbet, Miss Slater, George Ferrier, Irene McKay, David Rowland, Christina Ballantyne, Maria Maxwell, B. Todd, Mrs Swanston, and the driver, John P. Stewart. Minor injuries were sustained by Joan Jeffrey, Pat Paterson, Elizabeth Renton, Mrs Jean Purves, Mrs Janet Ellis, Mary Lorimer, Helen Dickson, Anna Jeffrey and Elizabeth Clark. David Rowland's life was saved by the badly injured driver, who managed to hold his head clear of the water. According to the *Kelso Chronicle*, 'Several of the passengers escaped with a shaking, and were able to proceed to their work.'